What I Tell Myself

ABOUT SELF PROTECTION

Written by Michael A. Brown · Illustrated by Ilham Fatkurahman

This book is dedicated to...

My children, Robert, Madison, Ava, and Amber. Your life is a gift from I Am That I Am. You have EVERY need to know how to protect yourselves. Your mother and I will not be here forever. You MUST survive. You SHALL survive. To adults, parents, grandparents, children, caretakers, crime victims, and others who want or need to take decisive actions of self—protection against active threats and deadly threatening situations but may not know how. Whether there's danger ahead or imminently present, it is NO ONE's job to protect you. It is your job. Be. Know. Do. Survive.

First Edition

Edited by Michele L. Mathews

Illustration by Ilham Fatkurahman

Design by Zoe Ranucci, www.GoodDharma.com

ISBN: 978-1-7341848-9-1

Library of Congress Control Number: 2020910583

There are lessons I must learn.
Parents can't be at every turn.

I MUST grow big and strong
If they are here or even gone.

It is NO ONE'S job to be
The one who can protect me.

Without delay
or sudden pause

I say these things
while standing tall.

6

I MUST do what keeps me free!
Safe and free from what hurts me.

Free to grow big and strong.
Free to live a life that's long.

Look left. Now right. Look forward. Now back.
Something's there? Don't point. Shhhhh. Stay back.

May be friendly. May not be.
Should I stay around to wait and see?

I might be afraid. I might be scared.
But I will survive. I am prepared.

I know myself
and what I can do.
I know how to call
9-1-1, too.

I'll shake a hand and make a friend.
I'll protect myself to the very end.

If I run, that is okay.
Live to see another day!

If I'm trapped by ANYONE,
I know it will NOT be fun.

15

I know I am in harm's way.
I WILL stand up proud and say

STOP means STOP!
NO means NO!

PLEASE don't grab!
PLEASE don't hold!

I speak peace to ALL life.
I speak peace. Don't want to fight.
PLEASE back up! PLEASE stay back!
Before you attack, I will fight back.

Something hard or with an edge.
I'll find it NOW. I'll have the edge.

I'll bust the glass. Kick the door.
I'll free myself! Say NO MORE!

Run fast and far away.
Tell myself, Death, NOT TODAY!®

I know when to stand my ground.
KNOW that I WILL stand my ground.

23

What I tell myself 'tis true

Who will protect me? I WILL, not you.

My Self—Protection Resources

Begin your research in finding the telephone numbers of the below resources that may be beneficial to you in helping you to protect yourself. Let's Get to Work!

Local Police Non-Emergency

Emergency Shelter

State / District Attorney

Substance Abuse Counselor

Victim Advocacy

Day Care

Suicide Prevention Hotline

Nearest Thrift Store

My Family Doctor

Nearest Hospital

Food Pantry

Therapist

Firearms Instructor

Transportation Information

Self Defense Instructor

Public Assistance Office

CPR First Aid Instructor

Allergies

Case Manager

Author's Note: Thanks, Ibriham for this idea.

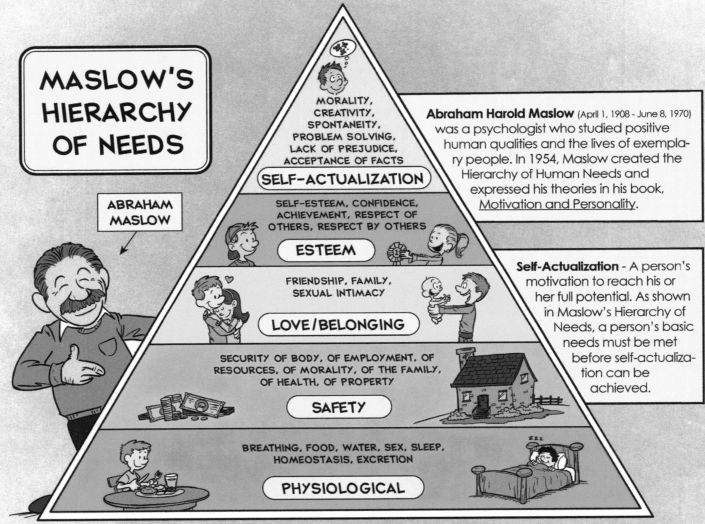

MASLOW'S HIERARCHY OF NEEDS

ABRAHAM MASLOW

MORALITY, CREATIVITY, SPONTANEITY, PROBLEM SOLVING, LACK OF PREJUDICE, ACCEPTANCE OF FACTS

SELF-ACTUALIZATION

SELF-ESTEEM, CONFIDENCE, ACHIEVEMENT, RESPECT OF OTHERS, RESPECT BY OTHERS

ESTEEM

FRIENDSHIP, FAMILY, SEXUAL INTIMACY

LOVE/BELONGING

SECURITY OF BODY, OF EMPLOYMENT, OF RESOURCES, OF MORALITY, OF THE FAMILY, OF HEALTH, OF PROPERTY

SAFETY

BREATHING, FOOD, WATER, SEX, SLEEP, HOMEOSTASIS, EXCRETION

PHYSIOLOGICAL

Abraham Harold Maslow (April 1, 1908 - June 8, 1970) was a psychologist who studied positive human qualities and the lives of exemplary people. In 1954, Maslow created the Hierarchy of Human Needs and expressed his theories in his book, Motivation and Personality.

Self-Actualization - A person's motivation to reach his or her full potential. As shown in Maslow's Hierarchy of Needs, a person's basic needs must be met before self-actualization can be achieved.

©Tim van de Vall

26

An Important Self–Protection Case:

Castle Rock v. Gonzales, 545 U.S. 748 (2005)
The United States Supreme Court is the highest court in the United States under the judicial branch of the United State government. Its decisions (holdings) become the law of the land.

The United States Supreme Court (the Court) granted certiorari to the case of Castle Rock v. Gonzales, 545 U.S. 748 (2005). The case involved a town's police department where its police officers failed to enforce a restraining order leading to the murder of petitioner, Mrs. Jessica Lenahan-Gonzales' three children by her estranged husband. Below is the holding and why self-protection is ultimately YOUR responsibility.

Question Before the Court:
Can the holder of a restraining order bring a procedural due process claim against a local government for its failure to actively enforce the order and protect the holder from violence?

Opinion of the Court:
No. In a 7-2 decision, the Court ruled that Gonzales had no constitutionally-protected property interest in the enforcement of the restraining order, and therefore could not claim that the police had violated her right to due process. In order to have a "property interest" in a benefit as abstract as enforcement of a restraining order, the Court ruled, Gonzales would have needed a "legitimate claim of entitlement" to the benefit. The opinion by Justice Antonin Scalia found that state law did not entitle the holder of a restraining order to any specific mandatory action by the police. Instead, restraining orders only provide grounds for arresting the subject of the order. The specific action to be taken is up to the discretion of the police. The Court stated that "This is not the sort of 'entitlement' out of which a property interest is created." The Court concluded that since "Colorado has not created such an entitlement," Gonzales had no property interest and the Due Process Clause was therefore inapplicable.

Castle Rock v. Gonzales." Oyez, www.oyez.org/cases/2004/04-278. Accessed 8 Jun. 2020.

An order of protection ALONE is NOT ENOUGH. You MUST take active measures to protect yourself and encourage your loved ones to do the same.

About the Author

Born in Chicago, IL, Michael A. (Mike) Brown, MA is the author of a revolutionary social emotional children's book series, What I Tell Myself, beginning with What I Tell Myself FIRST: Children's Real-World Affirmations of Self-Esteem. Based on Maslow's Hierarchy of Needs, this book of real-world affirmations highlights the various abilities and attributes of the reader while exposing readers to realistic possibilities of rejection of difference in various forms thereby enabling readers to form mental frameworks to surmount those forms of rejection and achieve positive self-actualization. Mr. Brown continues the mission to heal and empower all with What I Tell Myself About Self-Protection.

Mr. Brown is a product of the Chicago Public School system. He served in the United States Army and in various communities as a police officer. He is currently the President and Chief Executive Officer of MABMA Enterprises, LLC and the principal instructor of Security Training Concepts, a training agency specializing in collegiate / career occupational courses in multiple criminal justice and self-defense-related disciplines. Mr. Brown also serves as a nationally-certified anger management specialist and Crisis Prevention Institute-certified nonviolent crisis intervention instructor. He is the father of four beautiful children and believes in raising them into the best strong, capable, productive, responsible, and most importantly, happy human beings they can be. A former adjunct college professor and advocate of education, Mr. Brown is a graduate of Governors State University in University Park, Illinois, having been conferred a Bachelor of Arts degree in Interdisciplinary Studies (Criminal Justice, Psychology and Philosophy) in 2006 and a Master of Arts degree in Criminal Justice in 2012. He serves as an innovative and fresh approach to leadership, training, and empowerment and is a member of the International Law Enforcement Educators and Trainers Association, the National Anger Management Association, and the Society of Children's Book Writers and Illustrators.

Also from Michael A. Brown

What I Tell Myself FIRST *is on a mission to heal kids and parents!* ***Real-world affirmations WORK!*** Like the AED is to a heart, this book instills the defibrillator of self-esteem. So powerful that it addresses bullying and outside attacks on the self by other people who need the very same help themselves. For when times are tough and your mind is under attack, reality-based daily affirmations are the "I wish I had this" of books.

www.WhatITellMyselfFirst.com